Woodland Flowers
by Roger Phillips

assisted by Martyn Rix
and Jacqui Hurst

Elm Tree Books London

INTRODUCTION

Aim

In this book we have aimed to photograph and describe 92 of the commonest or more conspicuous woodland flowers found in the British Isles and Northern Europe.

How to use this book

The flowers are arranged roughly in order of flowering, from spring to autumn, and the date of the photograph is given on the caption. One photograph shows the most important parts of the plant, laid out so that details can be seen easily and clearly. The other shows the plant growing and gives some idea of its habitat, height, bushiness, stiffness. Sometimes, two closely related or similar species are shown together, and the distinctions between them are mentioned in the text.

What is a woodland plant?

Woodland plants have one thing in common; they can thrive under the shade of trees, in places too dark for most other plants. Many survive by flowering early before the leaves develop on the deciduous trees. Others, such as many orchids, flower later and are exceptionally tolerant of shade, and some, e.g. Bird's-nest Orchid and Yellow Bird's-nest, have become independent of light by being saprophytes. Others, such as Red Campion, are commoner in more open woods or shady hedgerows, which in many parts of the country are all that is left of former woodlands.

The Photographs

The studio photographs were taken on a bronica 120 format with a 75mm lens. Scale: ○ is 1cm. The field photographs were taken on a Nikon FM camera with a 50mm lens, occasionally with close-up attachments. The film was Kodak Ektachrome 64 ASA in both cases, but when used outdoors it was pushed one stop in development.

Bluebell wood

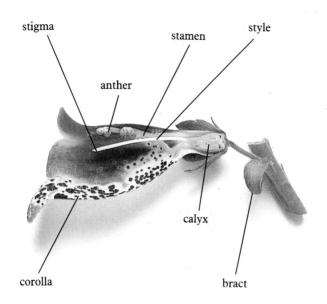

stigma

stamen

style

anther

calyx

corolla

bract

Glossary

apomitic	a plant in which seeds are formed without normal fertilisation taking place: the progeny are all genetically identical to the mother plant
lanceolate	shaped like a lance, wider towards the base
ligule	a thin piece of tissue at the junction of the leaf of a grass and the sheath
mycorhizal	specialised root infected with fungus
pinnate	with leaflets on either side of a central stem
rhizome	an underground, usually creeping, stem
sagittate	shaped like an arrow head
saprophyte	a plant which by possessing mycorhizal (see above) roots, can obtain its nutrients from dead leaves
septa	division within a capsule or hollow stem
stolon	underground shoot producing new plant
subsessile	with a very short stalk
tubercle	small, warty growth
umbel	many stems arising from same point, forming flat-topped head of flowers

Snowdrop photographed 16 February

Snowdrop photographed 16 February

Snowdrop

Galanthus nivalis, (amaryllis family), is among the first flowers of spring, opening in January or February and lasting 1–3 weeks, depending on the weather. On cold days the flowers remain half closed but in the sun the outer three white petals spread apart until they stand out horizontally, leaving the three small green-spotted inner petals to protect the pointed stamens and provide a hold for the bees which extract the pollen by vibrating the flower.

Snowdrops may be native in parts of western England such as along the Wye Valley where they are especially common in damp rocky woods, but in most places they have escaped from gardens into the wild; these escapes are often double flowered, with many extra green inner petals. On the Continent wild Snowdrops are found from France and Germany southwards to Italy, Greece and Turkey, and eastwards to the Caucasus.

5

Dog's Mercury photographed 19 March

Dog's Mercury photographed 19 March

Dog's Mercury
Mercurialis perennis, (spurge family), forms large dense patches of lush leaves, usually in dark woods or shady hedgerows, on chalky soil. It is common all over Britain, and is even found on mountain rocks in Scotland, although it is rarer in Ireland. The bright green young shoots often push up before the old leaves have died, opening their leaves and flowers to make the most of the light before the trees come into leaf. The male and female plants are separate and the former are easily recognised by their tiny green 3-petalled flowers with 8–15 prominent stamens. The patches are all of one sex and originate from a single plant; the pollen is carried from males to females by wind. It can be a nuisance in the garden, as it spreads underground by long runners. On the Continent it is found from Norway and Sweden, south to Spain and Algeria, and eastwards to the Caucasus.

7

Spurge Laurel photographed 18 March

Spurge Laurel photographed 18 March

Spurge Laurel

Daphne laureola, (daphne family), is very common in chalk and limestone woods from Lancashire and Northumberland southwards, but not in Scotland or Ireland. The small green flowers are likely to be overlooked as they are completely hidden below the leaves. They open in early spring and are faintly sweet-scented, attracting the bumble-bees and moths which pollinate them. If the plant is rubbed or bruised, or the flowers picked, their sweetness is overwhelmed by the acrid smell of the plant's poisonous juice. The purple-flowered **Mezereon** (*Daphne mezereum*) is deciduous and very rare in England, though common in some places in the Alps on limestone screes and in woods. It has bright orange berries, while those of Spurge Laurel are black. Both are poisonous. On the Continent Spurge Laurel is found from Belgium southwards to Turkey and North Africa, and in the Azores.

Stinking Hellebore photographed 18 March

Stinking Hellebore photographed 18 March

Stinking Hellebore or Setterwort

Helleborus foetidus, (buttercup family), is likely to be found in similar places to Spurge Laurel (p. 8), such as woods and bushy places on chalk and limestone, though it also thrives on sunny rocky slopes with some shade. It is an uncommon native in England northwards to Lancashire, but is found as an escape from gardens throughout England and Lowland Scotland. On the Continent it is found from Belgium southwards to Spain and Italy.

The leaves are evergreen, and the first warm days of January or February cause the flowering stems to elongate and the hanging flowers to open; bees visit them for their pollen and the nectar which is produced in tubular green pouches between the sepals and the stamens. Because of their very poisonous juice, Hellebores were formerly used as powerful purgatives, and are avoided by animals, even sheep and goats.

Green Hellebore photographed 19 March

Green Hellebore photographed 19 March

Green Hellebore or Bear's Foot

Helleborus viridis, (buttercup family), is an elegant but rare woodland plant, usually found on chalk or limestone soils, mainly in southern Britain, but it also extends as far north as Westmoreland. I have most frequently come across it in hazel coppices growing under oaks, along with Wood Anemones, Bluebells and Toothwort. The whole plant is deciduous, the flowering stems emerging shortly before the leaves, so that by flowering time (usually early April) the leaves are almost fully expanded. The flowers are visited by bees for pollen and for nectar which is found in curved nectaries, slightly longer and more numerous than those of the Stinking Hellebore.

The English Green Hellebore belongs to subspecies *occidentalis* which is found in western Europe from West Germany and Belgium south to Spain; the eastern subspecies *viridis* has hairy leaves and larger flowers and is found as far east as Hungary.

Lesser Celandine photographed 19 March

Lesser Celandine photographed 19 March

Lesser Celandine or Pilewort

Ranunculus ficaria, (buttercup family), is common all over the British Isles, Europe and western Asia. It is one of the earliest spring flowers, opening on warm days from January onwards in many different habitats, but generally in places which are shady or slightly moist in summer. The first flowers are usually found on sunny hedgebanks or on the sides of ditches, the surface of the petals shining in the sun, and attracting various insects such as flies and bees. The heart-shaped leaves usually emerge before the flowers, and provide valuable winter grazing for woodpigeons. The plant dies down early in summer and survives as a group of fleshy roots. The old name Pilewort refers to its former medicinal use when the roots were squashed, the juice mixed with wine (or urine) and the resulting mixture applied as a lotion for piles.

Primrose photographed 8 May

Primrose photographed 8 May

Primrose

Primula vulgaris, (primrose family), is one of the most characteristic plants of English woodlands and is found throughout the British Isles. In southern England it is only found under trees or on north-facing banks, but in the west of Ireland and in parts of Scotland it is common on open hillsides and grassy cliffs, as in these cool and moist climates the sun is seldom hot enough to damage its broad delicate leaves.

The flowers are of two kinds, pin-eyed with the style above the stamens, and thrum-eyed with the style below the stamens. For pollination to be successful pollen from a pin-eyed plant must reach the style of a thrum-eyed flower, and vice versa. The seeds are sticky when ripe and are attractive to ants which may carry them some distance from the parent plant.

On the Continent Primroses are found as far as North Africa and Turkey. In Greece especially the flowers are often pink or white.

Oxlip photographed 8 May

False Oxlip photographed 9 May

Oxlip or Paigle

Primula elatior, (primrose family), left, takes the place of the Primrose in parts of East Anglia from Essex to Norfolk and Huntingdon. It is characteristic of old woods, usually of oak with a hazel coppice on the boulder clay deposited by the retreating ice of the last ice age.

Its flowers are the same pale yellow as the Primrose, but are smaller and hang down to one side of the umbel. This is the best way to distinguish it from the **False Oxlip** (*Primula × tommasinii*), above, the hybrid between the Primrose and the Cowslip, whose flowers are larger, deeper yellow and hang down all round the umbel. Furthermore, the Oxlip is usually found in thousands, whereas the False Oxlip is found only in ones and twos, mixed up with Primroses and Cowslips near the edges of woods or on cliffs.

Oxlips are commoner on the Continent than in England and are found as far east as Russia and Turkey.

Sweet Violet photographed 7 April

Wood Dog Violet photographed 7 April

Sweet Violet, Wood Dog Violet

Viola odorata and *V. reichenbachiana* (violet family). These two Violets are the commonest species in chalky woods and are found all over Britain except in the far north. They are easily told apart as the Sweet Violet has deep purple or white flowers, sweetly scented, the Wood Violet pale mauve, unscented flowers. Sweet Violets flower from February to April, Wood Violets from March to May. The normal spring flowers are generally pollinated by bees, but both species also produce minute cleistogamous flowers in summer, which never open but still produce seed. The seed capsules of the Sweet Violet empty on the ground and rely on ants for dispersal but in Dog Violets the capsules are erect and when they shatter the seeds are shot out.

On the Continent Sweet Violets are found as far south as the Canaries and Palestine and Wood Dog Violet is even more widespread, extending east to Kashmir.

Wood Anemone photographed 7 April

Wood Anemone photographed 7 April

Wood Anemone

Anemone nemorosa, (buttercup family), is common throughout the British Isles and is usually found in woods, but sometimes also on sea cliffs or on heathy mountain sides, in places which may in the past have been wooded, but which have certainly been open for many hundreds of years.

The young leaves and flowers emerge together in early spring and the plant disappears in early summer, surviving by means of its fleshy underground rhizome. The flowers are usually white with some pinkish-purple on the outside of the petals, but may be pinkish, especially as they fade, or even pale blue. They are pollinated by beetles, flies and bees, attracted by the pollen. A related white-flowered species, *A. trifolia* found in woods in the foothills of the Alps and the Pyrenees, has long-stalked stem leaves with 3 lanceolate, toothed leaflets.

Yellow Wood Anemone photographed 10 April

Yellow Wood Anemone photographed 10 April

Yellow Wood Anemone

Anemone ranunculoides (buttercup family). This plant is easily recognised as it has a root and leaf like a Wood Anemone, but a yellow flower like a Buttercup. It is common in woods and grassy places in northern Europe, from southern Sweden, Finland and Russia, east to the Urals and south to the Caucasus and the northern Mediterranean, but is not found wild in England except as an escape from gardens.

Two subspecies are known; subspecies *ranunculoides*, the commoner subspecies, has a far creeping rhizome, whereas subspecies *wockeana*, from north-central Europe, is more tufted with a short rhizome and smaller flowers.

In places where the Yellow Wood Anemone, and the ordinary white Wood Anemone grow together the hybrid, *A.* × *lipsiensis*, may be found. It is intermediate between the parents with a creamy yellow flower.

Wood Sorrel photographed 11 April

Wood Sorrel photographed 11 April

Wood Sorrel

Oxalis acetosella, (oxalis family), is a very common plant found all over the British Isles in cool shady woods, hedgebanks and shady rocks even up into the highest mountains in Scotland. It can tolerate very deep shade and is often found growing among moss and feeble grass in places too dark for other flowering plants. The leaves have a pleasant acidic taste similar to its namesake Sorrel (*Rumex acetosa*), but should not be eaten in large quantities because they contain poisonous Oxalic acid.

The lilac-veined white flowers are produced in April and May, but apparently seldom set seed. As in the case of violets, seeds are formed by small cleistogamous flowers which do not open but remain hidden under the leaves and produce seeds which are dispersed by ants.

Wood Sorrel is found in Europe from Iceland and Norway across Siberia to Japan and as far south as central Spain and Greece.

Butcher's Broom photographed 23 April

Butcher's Broom photographed 23 April

Butcher's Broom

Ruscus aculeatus, (lily family), is striking for its green stems and tough spine-tipped 'leaves' which are actually flattened branches. The tiny purplish flowers which emerge from the middle of these leaves in early spring are usually unisexual, i.e. either only male or only female, but occasionally plants are found with hermaphrodite flowers which can fertilise themselves and so produce large numbers of shiny red spherical berries.

Butcher's Broom is frequent as a native in woods, mainly on the chalk and limestone and by the sea in southern England and Wales, but is found elsewhere as an escape from gardens. On the Continent it is common except in the north. The plants found around the Mediterranean often have narrower 'leaves' than those from the north.

Ground Ivy photographed 12 May

Ground Ivy photographed 12 May

Ground Ivy

Glechoma hederacea (dead-nettle family). This is a common plant of woods and shady roadsides, flowering in early spring from March until May. It grows best on heavy damp soils and is found, usually in masses, everywhere in the British Isles, except the northernmost parts of Scotland, and is common throughout Ireland. On the Continent it is found across Europe and Siberia to Japan. The flowers, which are pollinated by bees, are produced on short upright stems. The long trailing ivy-like stems, which have long-stemmed round leaves in pairs along them, are produced in summer, and in one season can extend to several feet. In very shady places the plant will grow but not produce flowering stems until it gets more light, for example after coppicing of the wood, or when the plant reaches the edge of a clearing.

Town Hall Clock photographed 2 May

Town Hall Clock photographed 2 May

Town Hall Clock, Moschatel or Five-faced Bishop

Adoxa moschatellina, (moschatel family). This whole plant lives up to its name, *Adoxa*, 'not outstanding', as it needs a keen eye to spot its tiny flowers. Until two other species were discovered recently in central China this was the only species known. Found all across the northern hemisphere, from Japan and North America, and as far south as North Africa and the Himalayas, it differs remarkably little over all this huge area. Its white delicate rhizomes spread underground to form quite large patches; its flowers face every direction and, although visited by various insects, they rarely produce their fat green berry-like fruit, at least in England.

It is found throughout most of England, Scotland and Wales, but in Ireland is known only in Co. Antrim, and is absent from the Channel Islands and the Isle of Man. It is commonest in moist woods, in hedges and on shady river banks under alders, but is also found among rocks in the mountains.

Goldilocks photographed 9 May

Goldilocks photographed 9 May

Goldilocks

Ranunculus auricomus (buttercup family). This is the commonest of wood-land buttercups, and the next to flower after the Celandine. It is usually found growing in small groups, particularly in damp woods, over most of the British Isles except the far north. Occasionally it grows in the open or on rocks.

The flowers vary somewhat in size and although many are perfect with 5 petals, others are likely to have some of the petals underdeveloped, or have no petals at all. Although visited by insects for the pollen, the plant is apomictic and produces seed without fertilisation. Flowering time is from March to May, and the whole plant dies away in summer to a short fleshy rootstock. It is unusual among the buttercups in that the leaves are not bitter-tasting, as its old name, Sweet Wood Buttercup, suggests.

Wood Spurge photographed 12 May

Wood Spurge photographed 12 May

Wood Spurge

Euphorbia amygdaloides, (spurge family), is common in woods, especially on rich, heavy soils, often growing among Bluebells or in damper places among Ramsons. The leaves vary greatly in colour, but are often purplish and contrast with the bright acid green of the bracts and flowers. New shoots are formed from the base each summer. They produce a rosette of leaves at their apex and the flower bud is formed in autumn to emerge quickly the following spring, the flowers opening in April. In England, Wood Spurge is commonest south of the Thames and the Severn, and is absent north of a line from the Wash to North Wales. It is very rare in Ireland, being recorded only along the south coast. In south-west Ireland, *E. hyberna*, a leafier, paler plant is common, but this is only known in England in the extreme south-west.

On the Continent Wood Spurge is found from Holland and Poland southwards to Turkey and North Africa.

Ramsons photographed 11 May

Ramsons photographed 11 May

Ramsons or Wild Garlic

Allium ursinum, (lily family), is common all over the British Isles, but absent from Orkney and Shetland. It is the only wild garlic which is found in woods, and it is easily distinguished from all others by its broad leaves. It is especially common in damp places in woods, such as along streams or in wet heavy soil, where it can cover large areas to the exclusion of all other plants. The leaves emerge in March, the flowers in April and May, and the plant has finished much of its growth before the trees come into leaf. The flowers are sweetly scented and their nectar attracts various flies.

On the Continent it is found from Norway and central Russia south to Spain, Turkey and the Caucasus. A second broad-leaved species, *A. victorialis*, is found in the mountains of Europe. Its leaves are more rounded, its flowers smaller and greenish yellow.

Bluebell photographed 8 May

Bluebell photographed 8 May

Bluebell

Hyacinthoides non-scripta, (lily family), is the characteristic flower of English woodlands in April and May. It is common all over the British Isles, usually in woods, but in the west often grows in meadows and on sea cliffs. It usually grows in great numbers and is especially conspicuous after woods have been coppiced, when the extra light causes it to flower even more freely than usual. The flowers have separate petals, but appear tubular, so are pollinated by long-tongued insects such as bumble-bees and some hover-flies. Honey-bees which have short tongues often visit the flowers, but steal nectar by pushing apart the base of the petals, and so avoid the style and stamens.

On the Continent Bluebells are surprisingly rare, being found only along the Atlantic Coast of France, Belgium and Holland, Spain and Portugal and very rare even as far east as Paris.

Bugle photographed 8 May

Bugle photographed 8 May

Bugle

Ajuga reptans, (dead-nettle family), is common throughout the British Isles in damp woods and is also found in heathy meadows. It has blue flowers rather similar to those of Ground Ivy (p. 30), but the two may easily be distinguished by their leaves. Those of Bugle are smooth and shiny, whereas the leaves of Ground Ivy are more rounded, dull and usually hairy. Bugle does not rely on seed for its propagation, instead it forms numerous long leafy stolons which creep over the surface of the ground and root at their ends, forming a new rosette of leaves and, in the following year, a flowering plant.

Bugle is found on the Continent from Russia south to North Africa and east to the Caucasus. The only other native blue-flowered species is the very rare *A. pyramidalis*, an alpine species found on limestone rocks in Co. Clare and Galway, in Westmoreland and in parts of Scotland.

Early Purple Orchid photographed 10 May

Early Purple Orchid photographed 10 May

Early Purple Orchid

Orchis mascula, (orchid family), is one of the commonest of all wild orchids, and the one most frequently found in woods. It is also common throughout the British Isles in meadows, or by roadsides, on both chalky and acid soils, flowering from April till June. On the Continent it is found throughout Europe southwards to North Africa and Lebanon. It can be recognised by its pinkish-purple flowers, which have a rather unpleasant catty smell, by its straight or upward-curving spur, and by its black spotted leaves. Only some of the Marsh Orchids (*Dactylorhiza* species) have purplish flowers and spotted leaves; they grow in wet places in the open, and always have spurs pointing downwards.

In the west of Ireland, especially on the Burren, and in the Alps, the Early Purple Orchid has unspotted leaves and grows in open meadows and on grassy ledges on the limestone, but the flowers retain their catty smell.

45

Wood Speedwell photographed 7 May

Wood Speedwell photographed 7 May

Wood Speedwell

Veronica montana (figwort family). Speedwells are most familiar as garden weeds or plants of sunny hedgebanks, but this species is found in damp woods and is common throughout the British Isles, except for the far north. It is thoroughly insignificant looking, and can be distinguished by its pale green slightly hairy leaves and trailing stems which are hairy all round. It flowers from April to June. The lax flower spikes with rather long (4–7mm) stalks to the flowers distinguish it from the Common Speedwell (*V. officinalis*), which is more frequently found in heathy places and in drier open woods.

On the Continent it is found from southern Sweden to North Africa, and east to the Caucasus.

Sanicle photographed 10 May

Sanicle photographed 10 May

Sanicle

Sanicula europaea, (celery family), does not look much like the more familiar members of its family, the *Umbelliferae*, such as Carrot and Hedge Parsley. The lower leaves are lobed, not finely divided, and the flower heads, which appear from May to September, are irregular, not the usual neat umbels. The fruits, however, are typical, and are covered in minute hooked bristles which attach to passing animals.

Sanicle is found in woods throughout the British Isles, but is commonest in beech woods on the chalk and on other rich soils. It also grows on shady rocks. On the Continent it is found in woods from Norway to North Africa and Syria, and even on mountains in the tropics in Africa, Asia and the East Indies. Other closely-related species are found in the tropics.

Lily-of-the-Valley photographed 30 May

Lily-of-the-Valley fruits photographed 10 September

Lily-of-the-Valley

Convallaria majalis (lily family). With their marvellously sweet-scented
flowers, Lilies-of-the-Valley are always associated with the beginning of
May in France. In Britain, however, they are not usually in flower until
mid-May, nor are they at all common, being found mainly in dry woods on
chalk or limestone, or sometimes in crevices or grikes in limestone
pavements from Scotland southwards, but not wild in Ireland. The plant
forms large patches, spreading by underground stems which run about
under the leaf litter, producing tufts of roots and aerial stems. The fruits
are large red berries, but they are not often produced in any quantity.

On the Continent they occur south to northern Spain, Greece and the
Caucasus region where several minor variants have been described as
distinct species.

Great Leopard's Bane photographed 10 May

Great Leopard's Bane photographed 10 May

Great Leopard's Bane
Doronicum pardalianches (daisy family). This conspicuous yellow daisy is not native to the British Isles, but is frequently found growing wild, having escaped from gardens, especially in Scotland and northern England, usually on shady roadsides, by rivers or in woods.

Another rather similar species, *D. plantagineum*, differs in having usually only one flower per stem, and in having upper leaves which taper at the base, and do not encircle the stem. It is also found as a garden escape and like Great Leopard's Bane, it flowers in May and June. As a native species Great Leopard's Bane is found mainly in western Europe as far east as the Alps, and south to Italy.

Cuckoo-pint fruits photographed 28 August

Italian Arum photographed 19 May

Cuckoo-Pint or Lords-and-Ladies

Arum maculatum, (arum family), one of the commonest spring flowers of woods and hedgerows, is found throughout the British Isles, except in the north of Scotland, and throughout Europe south from Holland. The actual flowers are hidden by the sheath-like spathe which is wrapped round the base of the rod-like spadix. Small dung midges, sometimes over a thousand, are attracted by the smell and fall down into the area of the flowers, and become trapped by a ring of stout hairs. Only after the female flowers have been pollinated and the males have shed their pollen over the insects do the hairs shrivel allowing the insects to escape.

Arum italicum has a yellow spadix, and leaves which emerge in autumn. As a native species (with all green leaves: subsp. *neglectum*), it is found only along the south coast of England. Subsp. *italicum*, which has white-veined leaves, is found along the western coast of Europe and the Mediterranean.

Herb Paris photographed 24 May

Herb Paris photographed 24 May

Herb Paris

Paris quadrifolia (lily family). This unusual looking plant is found in rich, usually damp, woods throughout England and eastern Scotland, but is absent from Ireland. The stems arise singly from a creeping rhizome, and have between 3 and 5 leaves; they do not always flower, but when they do, usually in June, the flowers are inconspicuous, having green pointed sepals and very narrow petals. The fruit is a black berry.

No other species of *Paris* is found in Europe, but there are several species in the Far East, some of which are grown in gardens. They are related to the Wake Robin, or *Trillium*, a common woodland plant of North America which has 3-petalled white or purple flowers and is often grown in European gardens. On the Continent Herb Paris is found from Iceland, Norway and Russia southwards to Sicily and eastwards across Siberia.

Pink Purslain photographed 19 May

Pink Purslain photographed 19 May

Pink Purslain

Montia sibirica, (purslain family), is native to western North America from Alaska to California but used to be commonly grown in British gardens and has escaped in several areas. It prefers very damp places, by springs and along tracks in rather open woods. It starts flowering in spring and continues sporadically until late summer.

Another species, *M. perfoliata*, also native to western North America, is commoner as a weed, especially on sandy soil in East Anglia. It has small white flowers, and its two-stem leaves have evolved to form a shallow saucer-like leaf from the centre of which the flowers emerge. The only native species of *Montia* is *M. fontana L.*, or Blinks, a tiny white-flowered plant common in marshes and ditches throughout Britain.

On the Continent, *M. sibirica* is not commonly naturalised, but *M. perfoliata* is found from Germany and Holland south to Hungary and France, and in Portugal.

Sweet Woodruff photographed 25 May

Sweet Woodruff photographed 25 May

Sweet Woodruff

Galium odoratum, (madder family), is the most common species of Bedstraw to be found in woods throughout the British Isles, mainly on chalk or
limestone, where it often forms large patches with its creeping underground stems. As the names Bedstraw and Sweet Woodruff suggest, the
plant was used as a strewing herb in medieval times. It is sweet-scented
when dried, with a faint vanilla-like smell.

Other species of Bedstraw are usually trailing and have long stems, with
similar whorls of narrow leaves at regular intervals. Sweet Woodruff was
formerly called *Asperula odorata* and may still be found under that name.
The only native *Asperula*, *A. cynanchica*, the Squinancywort, is characteristic of chalk and limestone turf in England and Wales and in western
Ireland.

Sweet Woodruff is found on the Continent as far south as North Africa,
east to Greece, and in the north to Siberia.

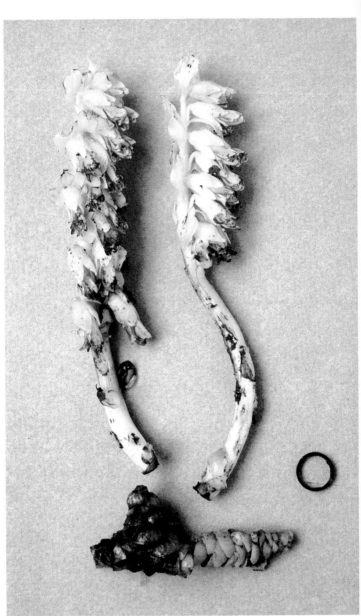

Toothwort photographed 9 May

Yellow Bird's-nest photographed 4 July

Toothwort, Yellow Bird's-nest

Lathraea squamaria, (broomrape family), is a curious plant that is parasitic on the roots of hazel or elm. It is found throughout the British Isles, except in the far north of Scotland, and is commonest on chalk or limestone soils. On the Continent it is found everywhere, eastwards to the Himalayas. Underground it has a scaly creeping rhizome, and the flowering stems appear in April and May. The plant has no leaves and no chlorophyll.

A second species *L. clandestina* with larger purple flowers is found on willow or poplar roots.

Yellow Bird's-nest *Monotropa hypopitys L.* (Monotropa family) also has no leaves or chlorophyll, but is a saprophyte. It is scattered throughout the British Isles, although it is very rare in Ireland, and is found mainly in beech or pine woods, but sometimes under hazel or in willow scrub in dune slacks.

Red Campion photographed 8 May

Red Campion photographed 8 May

Red Campion

Silene dioica, (carnation family), is common throughout most of Britain except parts of the west of Ireland. On the Continent it is found from Norway south to North Africa and western Asia. It is a familiar flower in shady hedgerows in late spring, and can be recognised by its bright pink flowers, and opposite leaves. It is also common in the less shady parts of woods among Bluebells in hazel or chestnut coppices. Like the Bluebell it is also frequent on sea cliffs, especially in the west of Britain, and it is said to enjoy the extra nitrate brought by sea birds.

The flowers are scentless and unisexual, the male and female being found on separate plants. Pollination is carried out by bumble-bees and hover-flies, which have long enough tongues to reach the nectar. White Campion (*S. alba*), which has pure white flowers, is a common cornfield weed.

Bush Vetch photographed 8 May

Wood Vetch photographed 6 July

Bush Vetch, Wood Vetch

Vicia sepium (pea family). **Bush Vetch** is very common along hedges and in open woods throughout the British Isles. It can be recognised by its dull mauve flowers, which open from May onwards and are in short-stalked bunches of 2 to 6.

Vicia sylvatica, **Wood Vetch**, is one of the largest and most beautiful of the vetches, forming large patches in woods and rocky places, and on cliffs and even shingle near the sea. It is found scattered throughout Britain, especially in Gloucestershire and Herefordshire, but in most areas is distinctly rare. It can be distinguished from other species by its very pale blue-veined flowers which are held in long-stalked racemes and are produced in succession from June. Tufted Vetch, *V. cracca L.*, is the most similar species, but it has rich blue-purple flowers and is much commoner, especially on roadsides or scrambling up hedges.

67

Herb Robert photographed 3 June

Herb Robert photographed 3 June

Herb Robert

Geranium robertianum, (cranesbill family), is found throughout Britain and on the Continent from Norway to North Africa and east to Japan. It is one of the smaller-flowered of the cranesbills, and is an annual or biennual with a single rosette of long-stalked leaves and flowers in pairs. It is common in woods, on shady rocks and in hedges, and a second variety, var. *maritimum*, is found on shingle beaches. A third variety, var. *celticum* is known from limestone rocks in Wales and in the west of Ireland, It has pale pinkish flowers and pale green, not reddish, leaves. Another species that is rather similar to Herb Robert, and might be confused with it is Shining Cranesbill, *G. lucidum*, which grows on shady rocks, on old walls and under hedges. It has less deeply lobed basal leaves, which have a shiny surface, and smaller, rounded petals.

69

Solomon's Seal photographed 24 May

Solomon's Seal photographed 24 May

Solomon's Seal

Polygonatum odoratum, (lily family), is the rarer of the two species which are found in the British Isles. It is found in woods on limestone, especially in north and north-west England, but also from Devon to Hampshire and into Wales. It flowers from May to June, and its petals are united into a long tube and are pollinated by long-tongued bumble-bees. The more common Solomon's Seal, *P. multiflorum*, is taller and has up to 5 flowers in each group, but the individual flowers are shorter, 9–15mm as opposed to 18–22mm long. It is found over most of England and Wales, especially on the chalk, but only as a garden escape in Ireland and Scotland. Both these species have blue-black berries. The common garden plant *P.* × *hybridum*, is a hybrid between these two.

On the Continent all three species are found from Norway south to Spain and the Mediterranean, especially in woods in the mountains.

Narrow-leaved Bittercress photographed 21 May

Narrow-leaved Bittercress photographed 21 May

Narrow-leaved Bittercress

Cardamine impatiens, (cabbage family), is more conspicuous for its narrow, jagged pinnate leaves than for its flowers which appear from May to August and are always small and may be without petals. It is a relative of the familiar garden weed, *C. hirsuta*, Hairy Bittercress or Jumping Cress, but is distinguished from this, and from the larger *C. flexuosa* by its tall, leafy stems and its narrow leaves which have sagittate basal lobes clasping the stem. The Latin name *impatiens* refers to the explosive seed capsules.

Narrow-leaved Bittercress is found in woods, usually of ash on limestone, and in Britain is definitely rare, although it has been recorded from Angus in Scotland south to Somerset and Devon. On the Continent it is known from Sweden south to Spain and Yugoslavia, and eastwards across Siberia to Japan.

Creeping Jenny photographed 18 July

Creeping Jenny photographed 18 July

Creeping Jenny
Lysimachia nummularia, (primrose family), is an attractive creeping plant that grows in damp places in woods, along tracks and streams and creeping under tall herbs in fens and lakes and by canals. It flowers from late May to August. The Latin name, *nummularia*, refers to the coin-shaped round leaves, and these and its much larger flowers distinguish it from Yellow Pimpernel (p. 76), which in spite of its name is also a loosestrife. Other large species of loosestrife, such as the Yellow Loosestrife (*L. vulgaris*), are tall and usually found in damp places, but are recognisable by their similar-shaped yellow flowers.

Creeping Jenny is found throughout most of Britain and Ireland, except in the far north, but in many places may be an escape from cultivation. On the Continent it is found from Sweden to Spain and Turkey, and east to the Caucasus.

Yellow Pimpernel photographed 18 May

Yellow Pimpernel photographed 18 May

Yellow Pimpernel

Lysimachia nemorum (primrose family). In spite of its name, this is a loosestrife not a pimpernel (*Anagallis*), though both are in the same family. It is the smallest of the loosestrifes, and its small starry flowers are very pimpernel-like. It can be distinguished from the true pimpernels by its seed capsules which split into five, not across the top. It is common in grassy woods and on damp shady banks throughout Britain and Ireland, but particularly in the west and north. It may be found in flower from early May till the end of the summer.

On the Continent it is found mainly in western and central Europe from Norway to Spain and east to the Caucasus.

Chickweed Wintergreen photographed 3 June

Chickweed Wintergreen photographed 3 June

Chickweed Wintergreen

Trientalis europaea, (primrose family), is a northern plant common in pine woods in Scotland but very rare in England being found only in East Suffolk, where it was probably introduced with imported conifer plants, and in the northernmost counties. As well as in pine woods it can be found on open moorland, sheltering in the moss under tall heather. The plant creeps underground through the moss by means of slender rhizomes, sending up, at intervals, stems with a rosette of leaves. The Scottish plants usually have dead white flowers, and this form extends across the whole of northern Europe and Asia. An almost identical plant, native to western North America, *T. latifolia*, has pale pink flowers, whilst *T. borealis* which is native to eastern North America has white flowers.

Chickweed Wintergreen is common in northern Europe, but found only in the mountains in the south as far as Italy and Romania.

Linnaea photographed 7 July

One-flowered Wintergreen photographed 7 July

Linnaea

Linnaea borealis, (honeysuckle family), was named 'by the celebrated Gronovius, and is a plant of Lapland, lowly, insignificant, disregarded, flowering only for a short while – named after Linnaeus who resembles it.' It is very rare in Britain, being found only in eastern Scotland, but is common in Scandinavia where it carpets the pine woods and its diminutive pink flowers scent the air in July and support swarms of mosquitoes. It is also found in the mountains in southern Europe, the Alps, Carpathians and Caucasus, and across Asia and into North America (var. *americana*).

One-flowered Wintergreen, *Moneses uniflora*, (wintergreen family), is another pine wood rarity, which is mostly confined to eastern Scotland, in the area of the Old Caledonian pine forests. It is, however, found across almost all the Northern Hemisphere and in the mountains in southern Europe, and in New Mexico.

Yellow Archangel photographed 18 May

Yellow Archangel photographed 18 May

Yellow Archangel

Lamiastrum galeobdolon, (dead-nettle family), commonly grows in woods
with Bluebells, and flowers at about the same time, but is found only in
England, Wales, southern Scotland and the south-eastern counties of
Ireland. On the Continent it is found from southern Sweden south to Spain
and east to Turkey and Iran. It is pollinated mainly by bumble-bees; the
lower lip forms the landing stage and the stamens and style, which are
protected by the hooded upper lip, come into contact with the hairy thorax
of the bee. The stamens tend to mature before the style, so, in theory at
least, cross fertilisation is assured.

Three subspecies are recognised in Europe; subsp. *flavidum* from the
Alps and Apennines has smaller flowers and long narrow bracts; subsp.
montanum has large flowers, 9–15 in a whorl, and subsp. *galeobdolon*
(shown here) also has large flowers, 4–8 in a whorl.

83

Sword-leaved Helleborine photographed 19 May

Large White Helleborine photographed 4 June

Large White Helleborine

Cephalanthera damasonium, (orchid family), is one of the commonest orchids in beech woods on the chalk, but it is also found on limestone soils from Somerset north to Yorkshire and Cumbria. It is easily recognised by its broad leaves and leaf-like bracts which are longer than the flowers, or at least the lower ones. On the Continent Large White Helleborine is found from Sweden and central Russia south to North Africa, the Caucasus and Turkey.

Sword-leaved Helleborine, *C. longifolia*, is less often seen than *C. damasonium*, but is more widespread, being found from southern England north to Invernessshire and in the Inner Hebrides, and in Ireland, where it is found in woods and in damp scrub, usually on the limestone. It is distinguishable by its narrower leaves, and its shorter bracts. On the Continent Sword-leaved Helleborine is found throughout Europe and Siberia east to Kashmir and Japan.

Lady Orchid photographed 18 May

Lady Orchid photographed 18 May

Lady Orchid
Orchis purpurea, (orchid family), is very rare in England and is found only in places on the chalk in Kent, though it was formerly also known in Essex, Surrey and Sussex. Even in East Kent it is much rarer today than it was about 20 years ago, as many of the localities where it was common have been cleared and ploughed. It is usually found in beech woods, but also in hazel coppices and on grassy banks among scrub. On the Continent Lady Orchids are still common in many areas, usually in scrub or on roadsides, from Denmark southwards to the Mediterranean and east to the Caucasus.

The **Military Orchid**, *O. militaris*, is rather similar, but has paler flowers and narrower lower lobes to the purplish lip. It is very rare in England, but commoner in open woods in Europe, especially in the Alps.

Fly Orchid photographed 7 June

Fly Orchid photographed 7 June

Fly Orchid

Ophrys insectifera, (orchid family), is one of the four British members of the genus *Ophrys* in which the flowers mimic female insects and are pollinated by male insects attempting to mate with the flower. Two species of solitary wasp have been observed visiting the Fly Orchid, and the lip of the flower resembles the back of the female wasp in colour and in the position of its hairs. The male wasps tend to hatch out before the females, and are attracted first by the smell of the orchid, which resembles that of the female wasp, and then by the similarity of the orchid flower to a female wasp sitting on a small green flower.

In Britain the Fly Orchid is widespread on chalk or limestone and is found as far north as Perthshire. In Ireland, it grows in woods, scrub and in fens, as well as in grassland; on the Continent, it is widespread except in the far north and in the south-east.

Greater Butterfly Orchid photographed 30 June

Greater Butterfly Orchid photographed 30 June

Greater Butterfly Orchid

Platanthera chlorantha, (orchid family), is especially noted for its sweet scent. It is usually found in woods, especially on chalk or limestone, but also on acid soils and in scrub or on grassy banks. It has been recorded all over the British Isles, except for the Orkneys and Shetland, and on the Continent is found throughout Europe eastwards to the Caucasus and into Siberia. The Lesser Butterfly Orchid (*P. bifolia*) is rather similar, but is commoner in the north and is usually shorter and found in more open and in heathier places. Its flowers are white as opposed to pale green, and smaller, 11–18mm as opposed to 18–23mm across. The two species also differ in their pollination; both are visited by night-flying moths which can reach the nectar in the long spur. Their stigmas, however, are in complementary positions, and cross-pollination is effectively prevented as the two species can be seen growing together without hybridising.

Common Twayblade photographed 7 June

Common Twayblade photographed 7 June

Common Twayblade

Listera ovata, (orchid family), is a common orchid in beech woods on chalk, but it is also found throughout the British Isles on calcareous soils and on old dunes, in scrub and in damp meadows or downland. It is easily recognised by its small green flowers, which have a long narrow forked lip, and the two large, opposite, parallel-ribbed rounded leaves which give it its common name. The leaves are more conspicuous than the flowers and can often be found growing up through beds of Dog's Mercury. The flowering period is unusually long, beginning in mid-May and lasting right until July or even August in the north. Lesser Twayblade (*L. cordata*), a moorland species, is one of the smallest orchids, with reddish-brown flowers.

On the Continent Common Twayblade is found throughout Europe from the Arctic across to central Siberia and south to the Mediterranean and Iran.

Herb Bennet photographed 18 May

Herb Bennet photographed 18 May

Herb Bennet or Wood Avens

Geum urbanum, (rose family), is common in woods and often grows as a weed in shady gardens, flowering from June to August. Its English name refers to its former herbal use and is a corruption of *herba benedicta*, 'blessed herb'. The root, which smells of cloves, was used to ward off evil and for keeping moths out of clothes. Like many woodland plants, the seeds of Herb Bennet are distributed by animals. Each has a long hooked spike on it which catches on animals' fur, or on human clothes. It is found throughout Britain, and on the Continent from Norway to North Africa and eastwards to Siberia and the Himalayas.

The only other *Geum* in Britain is the Water Avens, *G. rivale*, which has nodding, short-stalked flowers with brownish-pink petals and is usually found in marshes or by rivers or streams. Where a stream goes through a wood, fertile hybrids with flowers in all shades of orange may be common.

Blue Gromwell photographed 1 June

Blue Gromwell photographed 1 June

Blue Gromwell

Buglossoides purpureocaerulea, (borage family), is a rare plant in Britain, found mainly on the edges of woods on the limestone in Devon, Somerset and South Wales, and on chalk in Kent and Suffolk; it is in Britain at the northern limit of its distribution in Europe, and on the Continent it is commoner, especially in the south. It is found from Belgium and Poland south to the Mediterranean, Turkey and Iran.

Two other gromwells are found in Britain. Gromwell, *Lithospermum officinale*, is found in the same habitats as Blue Gromwell, but is much commoner, being found throughout England, Wales and Ireland, although it is rare in Scotland. The name *Lithospermum*, stone seed, refers to the nutlets which are white, shiny and very hard. It has small white flowers which appear in May and June. The other species, *B. arvensis*, also has small white flowers, and is a frequent cornfield weed.

Bastard Balm photographed 12 June

Bastard Balm photographed 12 June

Bastard Balm

Melittis melissophyllum, (dead-nettle family), is in Britain at its northern
limit, and is generally only found in the south, especially in Cornwall and
Devon, but also eastwards to Sussex, and in South Wales. It usually grows
in scrub, in hedges and in rather dry open woods. On the Continent it is
found most frequently in the south, especially in the hills. White-flowered
forms are found most commonly in southern and eastern Europe; purple-
flowered ones in western Europe.

Bastard Balm is sometimes grown in gardens, and its name links it with
Lemon Balm, *Melissa officinalis*, a common plant in old established
gardens. It is 'bastard' because it doesn't have the lemon scent of the true
Balm, but a stronger, unpleasant smell. Its flowers, however, are much
more beautiful than those of Lemon Balm and are pollinated by bumble-
bees and hawk moths. It flowers from May to July.

Honesty photographed 21 May

Honesty photographed 21 May

Honesty

Lunaria annua, (cabbage family), is always found in England as a garden escape, usually in hedges, by roadsides or on the edge of woods. It is a biennial, the seed germinating in spring and by autumn forming a rosette of long stalked heart-shaped leaves. This flowers the following spring, and by late summer the flat coin-like seed pods are fully formed. By Christmas most of the seeds have fallen and a transparent round membrane is all that remains, attached to the dead woody stem. Apart from the usual purple, a white and a variegated form are found in gardens which will come true from seed if kept separate from the purple form.

As a wild plant, Honesty is found in woods in south-eastern Europe, from Italy to Greece, but it is widely naturalised. A second, perennial species, *L. redidiva*, forms large clumps in damp woods, especially in the foothills of the Alps. The flowers are pale mauve, and sweetly scented, with oval seed pods.

Columbine photographed 15 May

Columbine photographed 15 May

Columbine

Aquilegia vulgaris, (buttercup family), is more familiar as a cultivated plant in gardens than growing genuinely wild but it is probably native in woods in most of England, Wales and Ireland, especially on chalk or limestone. On the Continent it is found from Sweden south to North Africa, and eastwards to Hungary. The flowers of wild plants are usually blue, but pink and white forms are occasionally found, especially where the plants are escapes from gardens.

The long-spurred flowers, which open in May and June, are adapted to pollination by bumble-bees. These can hang beneath the flowers and reach the nectar, but other insects often bite into the spurs and steal the nectar without pollinating the flowers.

A. atrata, which has blackish-purple flowers, is found in the Alps in woods and rich meadows, *A. alpina*, with large blue or blue-and-white flowers, is found in scrub or on rocks.

Small Balsam photographed 28 June

Small Balsam photographed 28 June

Small Balsam

Impatiens parviflora, (balsam family), is the commonest yellow-flowered balsam found in the British Isles. It is a native of central Asia where it usually grows on shady rocks, but here it is more likely to be found in woods or hedges, especially in East Anglia and around London, where it flowers from July to the first frosts.

The native, deep yellow-flowered **Touch-me-not**, *Impatiens noli-tangere*, is a rare plant of limestone woods, commonest in the southern part of the Lake District and north Wales, as well as the foothills of the Alps. Two other species of *Impatiens* are usually found by rivers. They are the large pink-flowered Himalayan Balsam, *I. glandulifera*, and the shorter orange-flowered *I. capensis* from eastern North America.

Wood Forget-me-not photographed 29 May

Wood Forget-me-not photographed 29 May

Wood Forget-me-not

Myosotis sylvatica (borage family). Like the Columbine, Wood Forget-me-not is more familiar as a garden flower or an escape, than as a genuine native. It is, however, found in great quantity in damp woods in some places, especially in central England, and here it is probably native. It is a biennial, or short-lived perennial, the seed germinating one year, and flowering the next.

It is distinguished from the Common Forget-me-not, *M. arvensis*, which may also grow in woods, by its larger flowers which are 6–10mm in diameter, against 5mm at the most in *M. arvensis*, and by its larger style which is longer than the calyx tube, rather than shorter as in *M. arvensis*.

On the Continent Wood Forget-me-not is found from Scandinavia eastwards to the Himalayas, and south to France and Turkey.

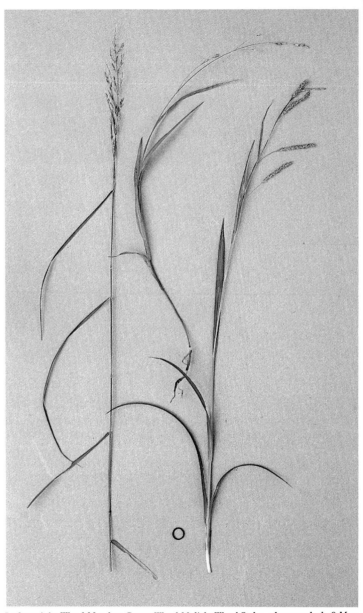

Left to right *Wood Meadow Grass; Wood Melick; Wood Sedge, photographed 28 May*

Wood False Brome photographed 10 July

Woodland Grasses

Grasses and sedges are essentially plants of open spaces, but a few are characteristic of shady places and woods. **Wood Melick Grass**, *Melica uniflora*, is found throughout the British Isles, often hanging down in masses on shady banks. The large-seeded chestnut-brown spikelets on a branched arching stem make this grass easy to recognise.

   Wood Meadow Grass, *Poa nemoralis*, is a very delicate plant common in shady places. **Wood Sedge**, *Carex sylvatica*, is a typical sedge, with male and female flowers in different spikelets, and a triangular stem, not a round stem as is found in most grasses. It is especially common in damp woods on heavy soil.

   Wood False-brome, *Brachypodium sylvaticum*, is common in drier woods. It is recognised by its broad drooping pale leaves and nodding head of large, many-flowered spikelets.

Tuberous Comfrey photographed 3 June

Tuberous Comfrey photographed 3 June

Tuberous Comfrey

Symphytum tuberosum, (borage family), is much smaller than the purple or
pink-flowered riverside comfreys, and forms dense patches in woods, in
shady places along rivers, and in hedges, flowering in June. It has been
recorded scattered throughout the British Isles, but is common only in
southern and eastern Scotland and occurs only very rarely in Ireland. The
only other dwarf pale-flowered species is *S. ibericum* from the Caucasus.
This is occasionally found as a garden escape, and has a slender, not a
tuberous rhizome. On the Continent Tuberous Comfrey is commonest in
the west and south. Two subspecies are recognised: subsp. *tuberosum* in
the west has short tubers, which are produced close together, and has 8–16
flowers in the inflorescence. Subsp. *nodosum* from the east, has smaller
tubers, more widely spaced and fewer flowers.

Foxglove photographed 16 July

Foxglove photographed 16 July

Foxglove

Digitalis purpurea, (figwort family), is commonest on acid soils, and is found throughout the British Isles in open places in woods, and on open hillsides, among rocks and on old walls, especially in the north and west. The plants are biennial. Each produces many thousands of seeds, so it can quickly colonise a suitable area, such as where a wood has been cleared or coppiced. The tubular flowers, which are produced from June until September, are pollinated by bumble-bees which crawl right into the flower. The bees visit the lowest flower first, which has usually already shed its pollen and has a stigma ready to receive pollen from the previous plant. The upper flowers have ripe anthers and the bees then transfer this pollen to the next plant they visit.

On the Continent the Foxglove is found mainly in the west from Norway to Morocco and east to Germany.

Larger Wintergreen photographed 30 June

Green-flowered Wintergreen photographed 30 June

Larger Wintergreens

Pyrola rotundifolia, (wintergreen family), is the largest and most beautiful of the wintergreens, of which five species are native to the British Isles. They are small but distinguished plants. Never common, they are least rare in lowland parts of Scotland, in pine woods and under heather, creeping through the moss-producing rosettes of rounded leaves and spikes of flowers. Found throughout Britain from Kent, where it grows in chalk scrub, to Scotland (Orkney), where it is usually found in mossy flushes on moors, or in woods, it flowers from July to August. On the Continent it is found from Scandinavia to central Spain and Turkey and east to Siberia.

Pyrola chlorantha, **Green-flowered Wintergreen**, is rather similar, but has shorter calyx-lobes 1.5–2mm as opposed to 2–4.5mm long, and yellowish-green petals. It is found throughout Europe, but is rare in the west, and absent altogether from the British Isles.

115

Common Wintergreen photographed 30 June

One-sided Wintergreen photographed 30 June

Common Wintergreen

Pyrola minor, (wintergreen family), grows in woods and on moors over most of England and Scotland from Kent to Caithness, and is scattered throughout Ireland. On the Continent it is found from Scandinavia to central Spain in the west and Turkey in the east, and across Siberia to Alaska and east to New England. It is distinguished from the other species by its very short style (1–2mm long), and its closed flowers with pinkish petals, which may be open from June to August.

Orthilia secunda is closely related to *Pyrola* but the small green flowers hang down on one side of the spike. The leaves are also different, being thinner in texture and toothed. It is found in Scotland and northern England and Northern Ireland, usually in woods or on mountain ledges, flowering in July and August.

Bird's-nest Orchid photographed 8 June

Bird's-nest Orchid photographed 8 June

Bird's-nest Orchid

Neottia nidus-avis, (orchid family), is frequent in woods throughout the British Isles, except in northern Scotland, but is often overlooked because of its brown colour which is similar to that of the dead leaves among which it grows. It does not require light for growth, being entirely saprophytic, and so can grow in the darkest places, in beech woods or even under laurels where no green plant can survive. It flowers in June and July.

It is the roots that are like a bird's nest; a dense bunch of blunt, fleshy mycorhizal roots are produced from a short horizontal rhizome. Only the flower stem appears above ground, and the first eight or so years of the plant's life are spent wholly underground.

On the Continent the Bird's-nest Orchid is commonest in central Europe, though it is found in the Mediterranean region, in Scandinavia and eastwards across Siberia.

Nettle-leaved Bellflower photographed 2 July

Great Bellflower photographed 5 July

Bellflowers

Campanula trachelium (harebell family). The **Nettle-leaved Bellflower** or **Bats-in-the-Belfry**, (left), is commonest in southern England in woods and hedges on the chalk, and has been recorded also in south-west Ireland. It flowers from July to September. **Great Bellflower**, *C. latifolia*, (above), is a more northern plant, common in woods and hedges on the limestone in northern England, and also found over much of Scotland. It is rare in southern England, but common along the Welsh border. The two species may be distinguished from each other by their lowest leaves, which taper into the stem in *C. latifolia*, and are heart-shaped in *C. trachelium*, by their flowers, which are larger and paler in *C. latifolia*, and by the difference in texture of the plants, bristly in *C. trachelium*, and softly hairy in *C. latifolia*.

Nettle-leaved Bellflower is common from Norway and Sweden to Greece and Sicily, while Great Bellflower is found mainly in central and eastern Europe.

Stinking Iris photographed 29 June

Stinking Iris fruits photographed 5 January

Stinking Iris or Gladdon

Iris foetidissima, (iris family), is common in southern England and Wales in open woods and in hedges, both on chalk and clay soils, and especially near the sea. It is found also as an escape from gardens in Scotland and Ireland. The flowers, which are usually purplish, but may be a dull yellow, open between May and July. The bright orange seeds are conspicuous in winter; they remain in the open capsule and are probably distributed by birds, though they have no edible flesh. The whole plant smells very acrid when crushed, though a faint whiff of the plant has been compared with beef, hence the West Country name Roast Beef Plant.

On the Continent, it is found only in western Europe from France to North Africa and along the Mediterranean eastwards to Sicily. Even in southern England it can be damaged in very cold winters, and this probably explains its absence in central Europe.

Common Cow-wheat photographed 26 June

Common Cow-wheat and Wood Cow-wheat photographed 29 June

Cow-wheats

Melampyrum pratense (figwort family). **Common Cow-wheat** is found throughout the British Isles, usually on acid soils in woods, heathy places and bogs. It has a long flowering period which can last from May to autumn and is morphologically variable, depending partly on the habitat and partly on the season of growth. The flowers are usually pale yellow, but may be almost white or deep yellow, and may have red or purple spots. The corolla is longer than the calyx lobes. **Wood Cow-wheat**, *Melampyrum sylvaticum*, is much rarer in the British Isles, and is found only in the north, normally in birch or conifer woods. The flowers are always deep yellow, but the short corolla distinguishes it from deep yellow small-flowered forms of Common Cow-Wheat.

On the Continent Common Cow-wheat is found as far south as Spain and Portugal, while Wood Cow-wheat is confined to the north, and to the mountains.

Hedge Woundwort photographed 20 June

Betony photographed 16 July

Betony, Hedge Woundwort

Stachys officinalis (dead-nettle family). **Betony** is common on shady hedge-banks and open heathy woods. It is easily recognised by its short head of bright reddish-purple flowers, which can be found from June onwards, and the stalked rosette of crenate leaves at the base of its stem. It is common in England south of Lancashire, but is rare elsewhere in the British Isles. On the Continent it is found over most of Europe except northern Scandinavia, and the Mediterranean islands.

Stachys sylvatica, **Hedge Woundwort**, is commoner than Betony and is recognised by its elongated spikes of dull dark purplish-red flowers, which open in July and August, and unpleasant smell. The whole plant is covered with rather bristly hairs which give it the appearance of a soft stinging nettle. It is found throughout the British Isles in woods, in hedges, on shady roadsides and as a garden weed.

Tutsan photographed 11 July

Tutsan photographed 11 July

Tutsan

Hypericum androsaemum, (St John's wort family), is a shrubby St John's wort found in damp woods and shady hedges throughout the British Isles, although it is most common in the south-west and fairly rare in the far north. It is also grown in gardens for its reddish fruits which turn black when ripe, rather than for its small yellow flowers. The name Tutsan is derived from the French *Toute-saine* (all healthy), and the leaves are slightly aromatic. It was confused by medieval herbalists with *Agnus castus*; this is a Mediterranean shrub which is strongly fragrant, and very different in leaf having deeply divided 5–7 lobed leaves and spikes of purple flowers. It was alleged to make men (and women) chaste, either when drunk or when branches were laid in the bed.

On the Continent Tutsan is found mainly in the west and south, from Belgium to Spain and Algeria and east to Turkey and the Caucasus.

Wood Dock photographed 16 July

Wood Dock photographed 16 July

Wood Dock or Red-veined Dock

Rumex sanguineus, (polygonum family), is the commonest of the docks found in woods, shady roadsides and other damp waste places. It grows throughout Britain, though less commonly in the north. The name refers to the uncommon variety var. *sanguineus*, in which the leaves have crimson veins and the whole plant is suffused with purple. Because of this colouring the plant was treasured by medieval herbalists and was considered useful for purifying the blood. The common wild plant can be distinguished from other common docks by its smooth-margined petals with one globular tubercle, the other two without turbercles, or with poorly developed ones. *R. conglomeratus* has three equal tubercles per flower and *R. crispus* has three unequal tubercles, but very wavy-edged leaves.

On the Continent *R. sanguineus* is found everywhere, as far south as North Africa and east to Central Asia.

131

Bittersweet photographed 18 July

Bittersweet photographed 18 July

Bittersweet or Woody Nightshade

Solanum dulcamara, (nightshade family), is common in wet woods, especially in fens, or by rivers or ponds, throughout the British Isles and Europe. It is also found on shingle beaches. The flowers are usually purple, with reflexed petals, and the anthers are held together in a cone, as are those of Snowdrops and Cyclamen. There are pores in the apex of the anthers, and the bees which visit the flowers vibrate their wings against them to shake out the pollen. The berries have a sweet taste initially, followed by a very bitter after taste, hence the name *dulcamara*, sweet-bitter. Each berry contains many small seeds. Geoffrey Grigson, in *The Englishman's Flora*, writes that the berries were often worn as charms, against witches, and that they were found, threaded on strips of date palm leaf, forming part of a colarette on Tutankhamen's third coffin.

Martagon Lily photographed 18 July

Martagon Lily photographed 18 July

Martagon Lily

Lilium martagon, (lily family), is one of the most widespread of all lilies, and is found from France, south to Spain, Portugal and east to Turkey, the Caucasus and across Siberia to Mongolia. It is doubtful whether it is native in England, though it is sometimes naturalised in woods, especially in southern England, flowering in late June and July. In the wild the flowers are usually pinkish-purple with dark spots, but in gardens white and various pinkish-flowered forms are common. The flowers are strongly scented, especially at night, and attract hovering moths whose long tongues can penetrate the narrow tubular nectary while their bodies brush against the dangling anthers.

One other lily species that may be found naturalised in Britain, particularly in Devon or in eastern Scotland, is the yellow-flowered **Pyrenaean Lily**, *L. pyrenaicum*. This is distinguished also by its many narrow leaves, not in whorls.

Left *Oak Fern*; right *Beech Fern*, *photographed 20 July*

Wood Horsetail photographed 2 July

Oak Fern, Beech Fern, Wood Horsetail

Gymnocarpium dryopteris, **Oak Fern**, is found most often in acid woodland under oak or birch, or in the open among rocks in the mountains. It prefers a moist, cool climate and is common in the north and west of the British Isles, but rare in the east and in southern Ireland.

Phegopteris connectilis, **Beech Fern**, often grows with the Oak Fern, usually in the same type of habitat. It can be distinguished from other ferns with similar frond shapes by its creeping rhizome which extends underground so that the plant can form large patches, and from the Marsh Fern, which also creeps, by its smaller wider leaves and its habitat.

Equisetum sylvaticum, **Wood Horsetail**, is found in the same places as the two ferns, but is commoner in the mountains and farther south in England, Wales and Ireland. Oak Fern, Beech Fern and Wood Horsetail are all found around the northern hemisphere to eastern North America.

Above *Golden-scaled Male Fern photographed 2 May*; below *Hart's Tongue Fern photographed 3 July*

Male Fern, Broad Buckler Fern, Hart's Tongue Fern

Dryopteris filix-mas, Male Fern, (not illustrated) is found throughout the British Isles, in woods, hedges and among rocks in the mountains. It grows on alkaline soils, as well as acid soils, where it may be accompanied by the **Golden-Scaled Male Fern**, *D. affinis* (*D. pseudomas* or *borreri*), which has golden-green young leaves and very scaly stalks, and by the Lady Fern, which differs by being more delicate, with the sporangia in elongated masses not covered by a kidney-shaped cap.

Dryopteris dilatata, **Broad Buckler Fern**, is also common throughout the British Isles, though to a lesser extent in East Anglia. It is found most frequently in slightly acid woods or on open hillsides in the north and west.

Phyllitis scolopendrium, **Hart's Tongue Fern**, usually grows in woods on limestone, in walls or on alkaline clay soils and is found throughout the British Isles, most commonly in the west.

Wood Sage photographed 14 August

Wood Sage photographed 14 August

Wood Sage

Teucrium scorodonia, (dead-nettle family), looks like a sage with its hairy wrinkled grey leaves, but smells quite different, rather pungent and reminiscent of hops. Indeed it was used for flavouring beer before hops came into common use. Early herbalists also used it as a diuretic, or made from it a tea against rheumatism.

Wood Sage is common throughout the British Isles, and on the Continent is found from Poland to Portugal and east to Italy. It is absent from Scandinavia. It grows in dry places in open woods, on rocks, among scrub or bracken, or on dunes, usually on acid soils though it grows on base limestone in the west of Ireland. It flowers in July and August, forming tufts of stiff stems about 30cm high.

The other British species of *Teucrium* (Germander) are rare plants of wet places, (*T. scordium*), or chalky fields (*T. botrys*) in southern England and Ireland.

Creeping Lady's Tresses photographed 5 August

Creeping Lady's Tresses photographed 5 August

Creeping Lady's Tresses

Goodyera repens, (orchid family), is a characteristic orchid of rather dry
pine woods where its rhizomes creep through the moss-producing rosettes
of leaves and vegetative runners as well as flowering stalks. The flower
spikes grow to between 10–25cm high and appear in July and August from
shoots which have built up a good rosette. After flowering the main plant
dies, leaving the vegetative runners to build up into new flowering plants,
which takes about eight years.

In Britain Creeping Lady's Tresses is found mainly in Scotland, especially in the north and east, and in East Anglia where it may have been
introduced with pines planted for forestry.

Other species of Lady's Tresses belong to the genus *Spiranthes*, and are
very different, being tufted plants with tubers and without creeping stems.

Broad-leaved Helleborine photographed 21 August

Broad-leaved Helleborine photographed 21 August

Broad-leaved Helleborine

Epipactis helleborine, (orchid family), is the commonest of the helleborines and is found throughout the British Isles, except parts of Scotland, growing in beech woods, oak woods, birch woods and pine plantations, on chalk, limestone, and acid soils. It is also found in the open, by lakes or on rocky hillsides and on the Continent it is found throughout Europe, in North Africa and east to the Himalayas. The rather dull, purplish-green flowers, which may be found from July to September, are very attractive to wasps, so are often cross-pollinated though they are capable of self-pollination. Other rarer woodland helleborines depend on self-fertilisation, and some indeed have cleistogamous flowers.

A second widespread woodland species, also cross-pollinated by wasps, is the **Violet Helleborine**, *E. purpurata*, a handsome, usually tufted plant that is found most often on chalky soils. It has narrower leaves, and whitish flowers.

Black Bryony fruit photographed 1 September

Black Bryony female flowers photographed 29 July

Black Bryony

Tamus communis, (yam family), is commonly found in England, and in Sligo and Leitrim in Ireland, on the edges of woods, in hedges and in scrub, especially on chalky soils. The twining stems, which can be 4 metres long, appear in spring from a large blackish tuber. Male and female flowers are found on separate plants, the male in stalked erect raceme, the female in sub-sessile recurved few flowered racemes; the flowers are open from May to July; the juicy orange fruits last well into the autumn.

White Bryony, *Bryonia dioica*, a member of the cucumber family, is another climber common in hedgerows in southern England. Here male and female plants are also on separate plants, but the flowers are larger, with 5 rounded petals. Both Black and White Bryony are known in the country as Mandrakes because of their large mysterious roots, though they are not related to the true Mandrakes. The berries of Black Bryony were said to remove blemishes from the face.

147

Enchanter's Nightshade photographed 1 September

Enchanter's Nightshade photographed 1 September

Enchanters Nightshade

Circaea lutetiana, (willowherb family), is a common plant in damp woods and a pernicious weed in shady gardens. It creeps underground with white brittle stems and soon forms extensive colonies. Like many woodland plants the fruits are small burrs, adapted to dispersal by animals. It is common throughout the British Isles, especially on rich soils, and flowers from June to August.

The name commemorates Circe, the beautiful enchantress who seduced Odysseus and kept him on her island for a year having changed his sailors into swine, though he himself was protected by the herb Moly (a garlic) given him by Hermes.

A second species of *Circaea*, *C. alpina*, is rare in woods in northern England and Scotland. On the Continent Enchanters Nightshade is found throughout Europe south to North Africa and eastwards to central Siberia.

Wood Black Bindweed photographed 18 September

Wood Black Bindweed photographed 18 September

Wood Black Bindweed

Fallopia dumetorum, (polygonum family), is closely related to the common Black Bindweed, but is not a weed and is larger and found in woods, especially those that have been coppiced recently, and in hedges. It grows mainly in southern England from Kent to Somerset and north to Worcester and may be distinguished from Black Bindweed, *B. convolvulus*, by its longer stems climbing to over 2m high, its long slender flower stalks, which grow to 8mm in length, and its shiny black fruit. It flowers from July to September.

It is rather like a small version of **Russian Vine**, *Polygonum baldschuanicum*, the rampant white-flowered climber which is often used to cover concrete garages and other eyesores, but that is a perennial with woody stems, whereas *F. dumetorum* is an annual.

On the Continent *F. dumetorum* is found throughout Europe and in western Asia and Siberia.

Orpine (subspecies maximum) *photographed 29 August*

Orpine photographed 3 September

Orpine or Livelong

Sedum telephium, (crassula family), is widespread throughout most of Britain and Ireland, but never common. The plant forms long-lived tufts from a bunch of tuberous carrot-shaped roots. The fleshy stems appear in spring and grow slowly through the summer, flowering from July to September. It is generally found in woods, scrub or in hedges on well-drained limestone or sandy soils. In England the flowers are always pinkish-purple, but subsp. *maximum* (left) has white flowers and is found on the Continent, especially in central and eastern Europe. Both extend across Asia to North America.

The name Orpine comes from the French *Orpin* or *Orpiment*, arsenic tri-sulphide, which was used as a pigment under the name of King's Yellow.

Ivy fruit photographed 5 January

Ivy flowers photographed 4 October

Ivy

Hedera helix, (ivy family), is very common in woods, hedges and on shady rocks throughout Britain, except in northern Scotland. On the Continent Ivy is found everywhere except in the north-east. It climbs up trees and forms thick ground cover in woods as its evergreen leaves can tolerate the dense shade cast by deciduous trees. The plant exhibits two distinct forms, a trailing or climbing form which roots as it goes or clings to trees by aerial roots, and a shrubby or aborescent form which makes a dense bush that flowers when it has sufficient light. The climbing form turns into the shrubby form when it reaches the top of a wall or tree, but if cuttings are taken of the shrubby form, they remain shrubby.

The green flowers of Ivy are among the last to open in autumn, and provide a good supply of nectar for a variety of insects, especially wasps and flies. The berries, which are black, ripen in spring.

Mistletoe fruit photographed 23 December

Mistletoe photographed 19 March

Mistletoe

Viscum album, (mistletoe family), forms the familiar green 'birds' nests' in trees, usually poplar, lime or apple, and very rarely oak. It is a parasite and lacks roots but has special suckers (haustoria) which spread for a short distance under the bark of the host tree, making use of its sap, from which it gets water and mineral salts. It does not require carbohydrates from the host, as do other parasites such as Broomrape, Dodder or parasitic fungi, because these can be made by the Mistletoe's own chlorophyll.

Mistletoe has long been associated with magic, especially with fertility, and in England is rarely very common, though it is most frequent south of London, and around the Severn Valley. It is not known in Ireland. In parts of France, however, it can be seen in great quantity, especially on old apple trees, and elsewhere on the Continent it is found everywhere except in the far north.

INDEX

Roger Phillips has pioneered the photography of natural history which ensures reliable identification. By placing each specimen against a plain background he is able to show details that would otherwise have been lost if it had been photographed solely *in situ*. Such is the success of his technique that his books, which include the definitive guide to *Mushrooms* and *Wild Food*, have sold over a million copies worldwide. He is also the winner of numerous awards, including three for best produced and best designed books and the André Simon prize for 1983 for *Wild Food*.

Martyn Rix took a degree in botany at Trinity College, Dublin and then went on to Cambridge. After a further period of study in Zurich he became resident botanist at the Royal Horticultural Society's gardens at Wisley for several years. He is now a freelance writer.

Jacqui Hurst studied photography at Gloucestershire College of Art & Design, worked as an assistant to Roger Phillips for 4 years, and is now a freelance journalist and photographer, specialising in country matters.

Acknowledgements
We should like to thank John & Caroline Stevenson for their help in finding many of the plants photographed here.

First published in Great Britain 1986
by Elm Tree Books/Hamish Hamilton Ltd
Garden House 57-59 Long Acre London WC2E 9JZ

Cover design by Pat Doyle

British Library Cataloguing in Publication Data

Phillips, Roger, *1932*–
    Woodland flowers.
    1. Forest flora – Identification
    I. Title   II. Rix, Martyn   III. Hurst, Jacqui
    582.13   QK938.F6
    ISBN 0-241-11813-1
    ISBN 0-241-11757-7 Pbk

Typeset by Rowland Phototypesetting Ltd, Bury St Edmunds, Suffolk
Printed and bound in Italy by
Arnoldo Mondadori Editore, Verona